Ways into Science

Your Body, Your Senses

Peter Riley

W
FRANKLIN WATTS
LONDON•SYDNEY

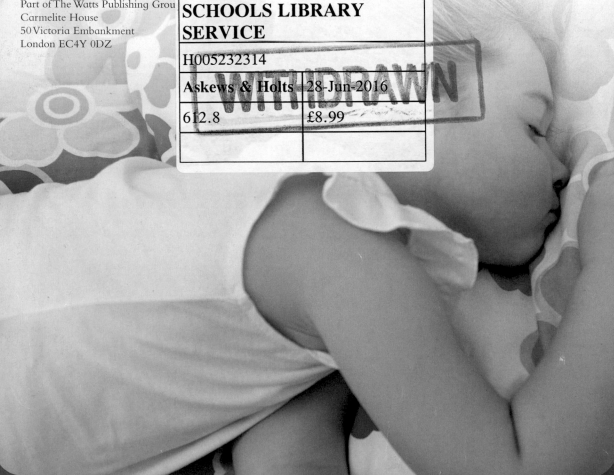

Franklin Watts
Published in Great Britain in 2016
by The Watts Publishing Group

Copyright images © Franklin Watts 2014
Copyright text © Peter Riley 2014
(Text has previously appeared in Ways into Science:
Senses (2001) but has been comprehensively
re-written for this edition.)

Editor: Julia Bird
Designer: Basement 68

ISBN: 978 1 4451 3479 6
Dewey classification number: 573.87

Printed in China

Franklin Watts
An imprint of
Hachette Children's Group
Part of The Watts Publishing Grou
Carmelite House
50 Victoria Embankment
London EC4Y 0DZ

An Hachette UK Company
www.hachette.co.uk
www.franklinwatts.co.uk

Photo acknowledgements: Alvera/Dreamstime: 10bl. Artmim/
Dreamstime: 15b. Laura Nadina Colvalcuic/Dreamstime:
13bl. Mihail Degteariov/Dreamstime: 22bl. Elena Elisseev/
Dreamstime: 14bc. Martin Fischer/Dreamstime: 5tr, 15t.
Steven Frame/Dreamstime: front cover t. Gelpi/Dreamstime:
7b. Erin Janssen/Dreamstime: 12t. Micha Klootwijk/Dreams-
time: 12c. Susan Leggett/Dreamstime: 7c, 10t. Pavel Losevsky/
Dreamstime: 13t. Alena Ozerova/Dreamstime: 8. Horst
Petzoid/Dreamstime: 7t. Boris Ryaposov/Dreamstime: 4, 24b.
Serrnovik/Dreamstime: 6. Yury Shirokov/Dreamstime: 5cr, 14t.
Willeecole/Dreamstime: 19b. Wollemipine/Dreamstime: 5crb,
10br. Matthias Zeigler/Dreamstime: 5br, 14bl.
Every attempt has been made to clear copyright.
Should there be any inadvertent omission,
please apply to the Publishers for rectification.

FSC
www.fsc.org
MIX
Paper from
responsible sources
FSC® C104740

Contents

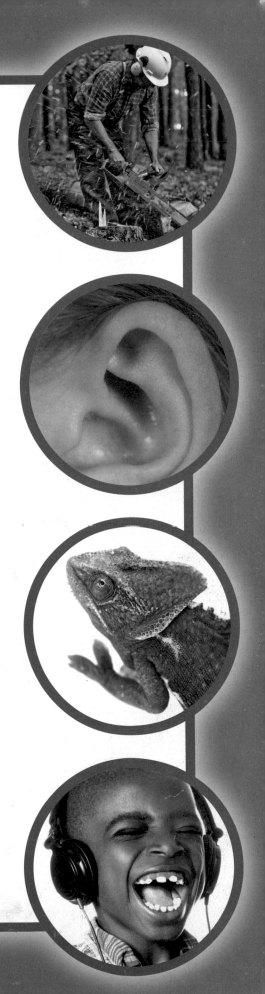

Parts of the body

Our body has many parts.

hair

head

neck

shoulder

ribs

elbow

arm

skin

hand

fingers

knee

leg

toes

foot

Some parts of our body help us sense the world around us.

They tell us if something smells.

They tell us if it is light or dark.

They tell us if it is loud or quiet.

Do you know what these body parts are? They help us to use our senses. Turn the page to find out all about our senses.

7

our senses

Our body and our senses
work together to tell us
about the world.

We use our sense of
sight to see things.

We use our sense of hearing to hear things.

We use our sense of smell to smell things.

We use our sense of taste to taste things.

We use our sense of touch to feel things.

What can you sense right now?

Sight

Our eyes give us our sense of sight.

Your eyes can only see what is in front of you.

A chameleon can turn its eyes in different directions so it can see all around.

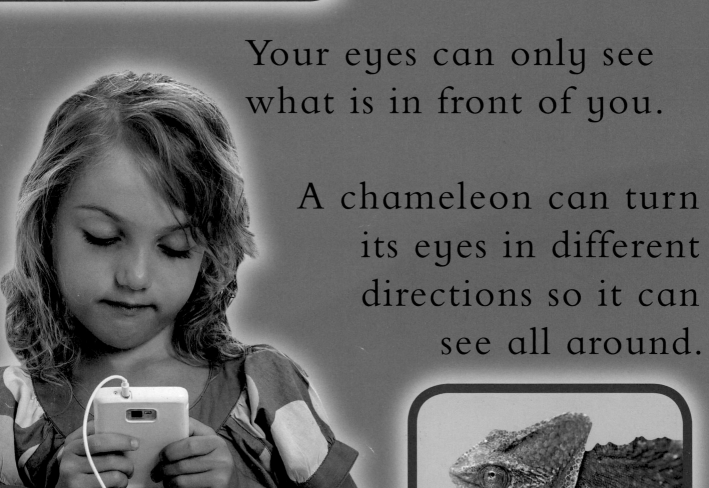

We can see different colours. How many colours can you see on Ben's T-shirt?

We can see things that are near.

We can also see things that are far away.

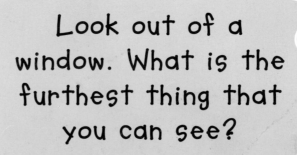

Look out of a window. What is the furthest thing that you can see?

11

Light in the eye

We see things when light goes into our eyes. It goes through a hole called a pupil.

Our pupils can change size. When it is bright, our pupils are smaller.

Hannah is in bright light. Her pupils are small.

When it is darker, our pupils grow bigger. They let in more light to help us see.

Hannah sits in a shady place. Her pupils have become big.

The iris is the coloured ring around the pupil. It has muscles that make the pupil change size.

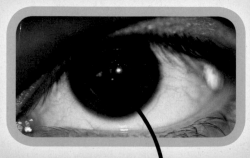

This is a brown iris.

What colour are your irises?

13

Hearing

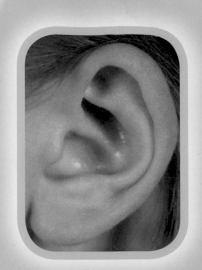

Our ears give us our sense of hearing. We can hear sounds all around our body.

Jake can hear music on his headphones.

Katie can hear a door closing behind her.

We can hear loud sounds clearly.

Loud sounds can hurt our ears. People who work in very noisy places wear ear protectors.

Quiet sounds, like rustling leaves, can be difficult to hear.

Sally puts her hand around her ear to listen to the rustling leaves. What do you think happens? Turn the page to find out.

Hearing test

Sally can hear the leaves rustling more clearly. Try cupping your hands around your ears to hear a noise better.

Here is another hearing game.

Raj sits on a chair and puts on a blindfold.

Laura has two coins.

Laura stands near Raj.
She clicks the coins together.

Raj points
to where
he thinks
Laura is.

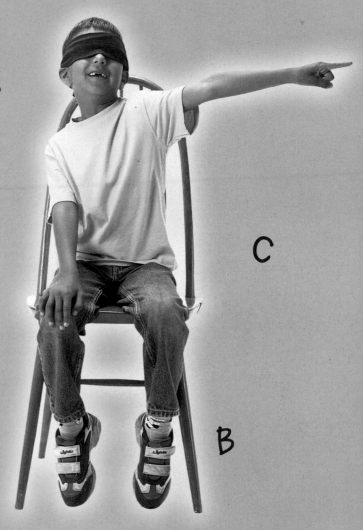

C

A

B

Laura moves to place A, B and C
and clicks the coins each time. Raj
gets better at guessing where she is.

Try Laura's test on your friends.

Smell

Our nose gives us our sense of smell.

All sorts of things can be smelled.

Matthew can smell the scent of a flower.

Hannah can smell shoe polish.

Some smells are pleasant.

Some smells are unpleasant!

Dogs need a better sense of smell than humans. Can you think why?

19

Smell test

Sam has some clean, empty yoghurt pots.

He puts a different piece of food in each one.

Sam covers each pot with kitchen towel.

20

Sam gives a yoghurt
pot to Nicole.

Nicole sniffs the top of the pot.

She uses her sense of smell
to guess what the food is.

Nicole tries all the pots.

Is it apple?

Try Sam's
test on your friends.

Five tastes

Our tongue gives us our sense of taste. We use it to tell our body about our food and drink.

Everyone has a different sense of taste.

Laura likes strawberries.

Raj does not.

Our tongues can tell five different tastes. These are: sweet, savoury, salty, sour and bitter.

Paul has some foods with different tastes.

vinegar

jam

lemon

salty crisps

sweets

coffee

bacon

Which taste do you think each one has?

23

Touch

Our skin covers
our body. It gives
us our sense of touch.

We can feel a hard floor
with our bare feet.

We can feel the softness of
a pillow with our face.

We mainly use our fingers to touch things.

Things can feel rough or smooth.

Sandpaper feels rough.

An apple's skin feels smooth.

Things can feel warm or cold.

This cup feels warm.   This glass feels cold.

Touch test

Raj puts an apple in a bag. He gives the bag to Katie.

Katie feels in the bag.

Katie guesses what the object is. She checks to see if she is right.

Try this test on your friends.

Using your senses

We use our senses all the time.
We often use them together.

Make a table like this
one. Put a tick next to
the senses you use.

activity	sight	hearing	smell	taste	touch
cross a road	✓	✓	✗	✗	✗
play on a computer	?	?	?	?	?
enjoy a meal	?	?	?	?	?
play catch	?	?	?	?	?

Think of some other activities.
Add them to your table.

Useful words

Chameleon – a member of the reptile group of animals that can change the colour of its body.

Elbow – the joint between the bones of the upper and lower arm.

Headphones – speakers that fit over the ears. You must not make the sound too loud because it will harm your ears.

Iris – a coloured ring in the eye around the pupil that is made of muscle.

Knee – the joint between the bones of the upper and lower leg.

Muscles – parts of the body that make things move.

Pupil – the black hole in the centre of the eye through which light passes.

Shady – a place where there are shadows and the light is dim.

Tongue – a part of the mouth that helps us taste food and swallow it.

Some answers

Here are some answers to the questions we have asked in this book. Don't worry if you had some different answers to ours: you may be right, too. Talk through your answers with other people and see if you can explain why they are right.

Page 7 Nose, eyes and ears.

Page 9 You are using your sense of sight to read this book and sense of touch to feel its pages.

Page 11 Ben's T-shirt has five colours (blue, red, black, white and orange).

Page 13 Your irises may be blue, brown, grey-blue or green.

Page 19 Dogs need a strong sense of smell to find food as they cannot see as well as us.

Page 27 When you cross a road you use sight and hearing; when you play on a computer you use sight, hearing and touch; when you enjoy a meal you use sight, smell, touch and taste; when you play catch you use sight and touch.

Index

About this book

Ways into Science is designed to encourage children to think about their everyday world in a scientific way and to make investigations to test their ideas. There are five lines of enquiry that scientists make in investigations. These are grouping and classifying, observing over time, making a fair test, searching for patterns and researching using secondary sources.

• When children open this book they are already making one line of enquiry – researching about the body and senses. As they read through the book they are invited to make other lines of enquiry and to develop skills in scientific investigation.

• On page 23 they are asked to group and classify.

• On pages 9, 11, 13, 17, 21 and 26 they are invited to try out their observational skills.

• On page 15 they are asked to make a prediction.

• On pages 17, 21 and 26 they are challenged to perform simple tests and carry out investigations.

• On pages 17, 21 and 26 they can draw conclusions from their investigations.

• On page 27 they are invited to construct a table and fill it in.